Dear Reader,

In 2012, my family and I took a summer vacation to Montana, Wyoming, and South Dakota. One of our stops was Yellowstone National Park. Journeying through the park, I was in awe of the spurting geysers, gurgling mud pots, and colorful hot springs. As an elementary school teacher, when I discovered these incredible sites were created by a volcano lying below the park, I knew I had to share these wonders with my students.

That year, I transformed my classroom into a miniature Yellowstone and immersed my students in books, videos, and projects revolving around the park. This was a new method of teaching for me, and it sparked a fire under my students by motivating and engaging them. Now retired, I have the privilege of sharing the wonders of Yellowstone with you.

Enjoy learning about Yellowstone's amazing water features, animals, plants, and, of course, its supervolcano. I hope you take the pledge at the end of the book to become a steward of not only Yellowstone but also our beautiful planet. The world could use more superheroes championing the need to keep our environment clean, our animals protected, and our planet preserved for future generations.

Suzanne Jacobs Lipshaw

The Super Volcano: A Hidden Hero Below Yellowstone National Park
Hardcover first edition · November 2024 · ISBN: 978-1-958629-57-4
Paperback first edition · May 2025 · ISBN: 978-1-958629-78-9
eBook first edition · November 2024 · ISBN: 978-1-958629-58-1

Written by Suzanne Jacobs Lipshaw, Text © 2024
Illustrated by Brie Schmida, Illustrations © 2024

Project Manager, Cover and Book Design: Hannah Thelen, Washington, D.C.
Editors: Caitlin Burnham, Washington, D.C.
          Violet Antonick, Washington, D.C.
Editorial Assistants:
          Brooke McGurl
          Jordan Roller
          Marlee Brooks

Available in Spanish as El super volcán: Un héroe oculto debajo del Parque Nacional de Yellowstone
Spanish paperback first edition · May 2025 · ISBN: 978-1-958629-79-6
Spanish eBook first edition · May 2025 · ISBN: 978-1-958629-80-2

Teacher's Guide available at the Educational Resources page of ScienceNaturally.com.

Published by:
Science, Naturally! - An imprint of Platypus Media, LLC
    750 First Street NE, Suite 700
    Washington, DC 20002
    202-465-4798
    Info@ScienceNaturally.com · ScienceNaturally.com

Distributed to the book trade by:
    Baker & Taylor Publisher Services (North America)
    Toll-free: (888) 814 0208
    Orders@BTPubServices.com · BTPubServices.com

Library of Congress Control Number: 2024935657

10 9 8 7 6 5 4 3 2 1

Schools, libraries, government and non-profit organizations can receive a bulk discount for quantity orders.
Contact us at Info@ScienceNaturally.com for more information.

The front cover may be reproduced freely, without modification, for review or non-commercial educational purposes.

All rights reserved. No part of this book may be reproduced in any form without the express written permission of the publisher. Front cover exempted (see above).

Printed in China.

To Marc,

For journeying with me to wondrous places and throughout life.

—Suzanne Jacobs Lipshaw

To Grammy and Papa,

For all the creek adventures, prayers, and love poured out on a grateful little granddaughter.

—Brie Schmida

The SUPER VOLCANO

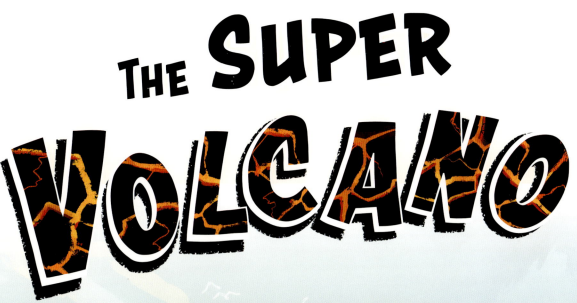

A HIDDEN HERO BELOW YELLOWSTONE NATIONAL PARK

BY SUZANNE JACOBS LIPSHAW
ILLUSTRATED BY BRIE SCHMIDA

Science, Naturally!
An imprint of Platypus Media, LLC
Washington, D.C.

BENEATH YELLOWSTONE NATIONAL PARK SIMMERS A SUPERHERO.

ITS POWERS?

AND CREATING WONDROUS

WATER DISPLAYS!

Yellowstone showcases the largest collection of *hydrothermal* features on Earth. Artfully crafted by rainwater and snow that has been superheated by the blistering rock below, Yellowstone's *geysers*, *hot springs*, *mud pots*, and *fumaroles* fascinate park visitors year round.

THE HERO'S MIGHTY FEATS INCLUDE...

Below Yellowstone is a web of cracks that acts like a plumbing system. Hot water rises through the cracks and is sometimes trapped by a rocky clog. When pressure builds, the water bursts through the clog, erupting into a tower of scalding water and sizzling steam.

GLOOP!

Mud pots are made when water mixes with *sulfuric acid* underground. This mixture breaks down rocks, turning them into a murky clay pool. When steam and gases escape, the mud pots bubble and burp. Since sulfur smells like rotten eggs, mud pots are the stinkiest sites in the park.

Fumaroles are sometimes called dry geysers because there's barely any water below them. The water that is there boils away from the intense heat, transforming into steam. The scorching steam then pushes through the fumarole's plumbing system, shooting out into the hottest hydrothermal feature in Yellowstone.

HISSS!

HISSS!

Hot springs are pools of heated water that easily rise through the underground cracks below Yellowstone. The most common *thermal* feature, they can be a brilliant blue or a palette of colorful rings. Despite how refreshing they look, the hot springs in Yellowstone are way too hot for swimming!

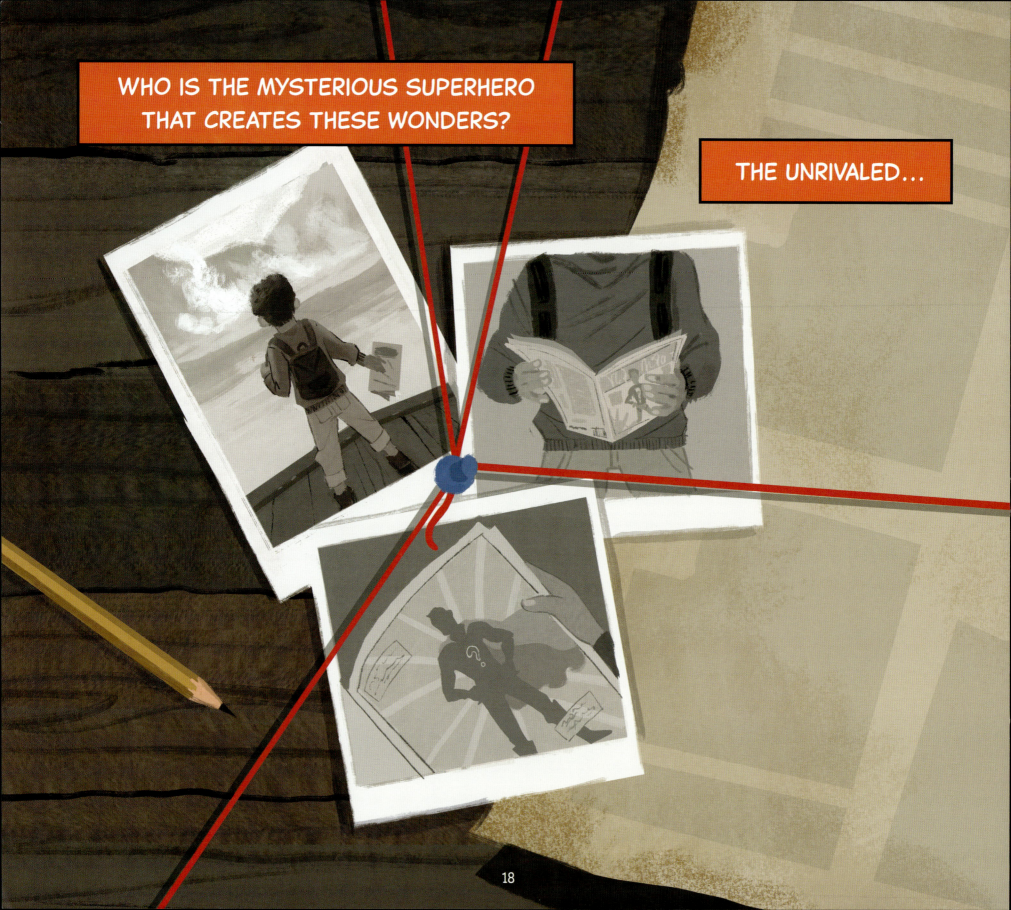

YELLOWSTONE SUPERVOLCANO!

Yellowstone National Park sits atop a giant sleeping volcano.

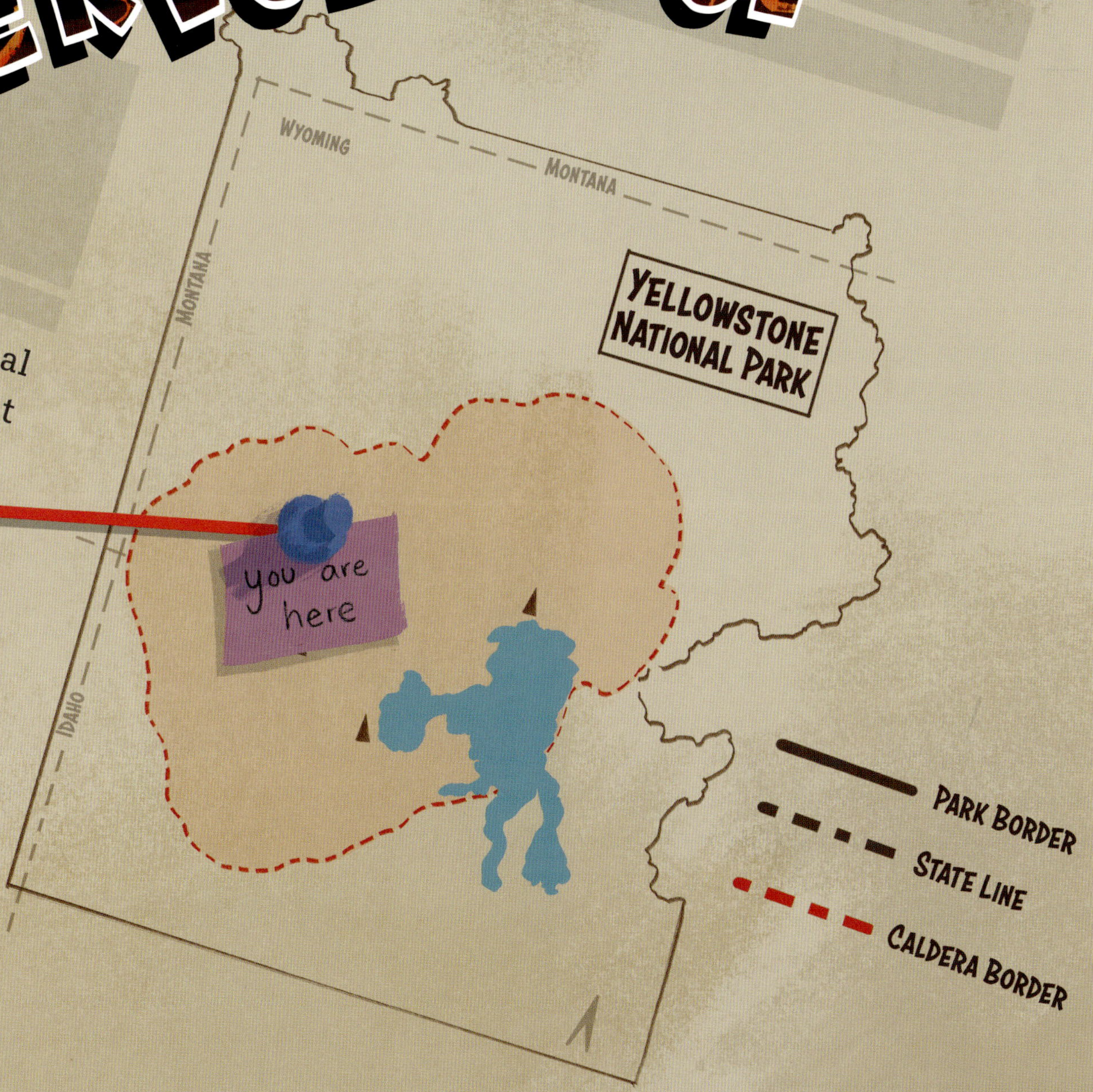

Unlike other volcanoes, you can't really see the Yellowstone Supervolcano, even from above. About 631,000 years ago, a huge **eruption** caused the volcano to collapse in on itself, creating an enormous crater known as the Yellowstone Caldera.

WYOMING

MONTANA

MONTANA

IDAHO

YELLOWSTONE NATIONAL PARK

you are here

PARK BORDER

STATE LINE

CALDERA BORDER

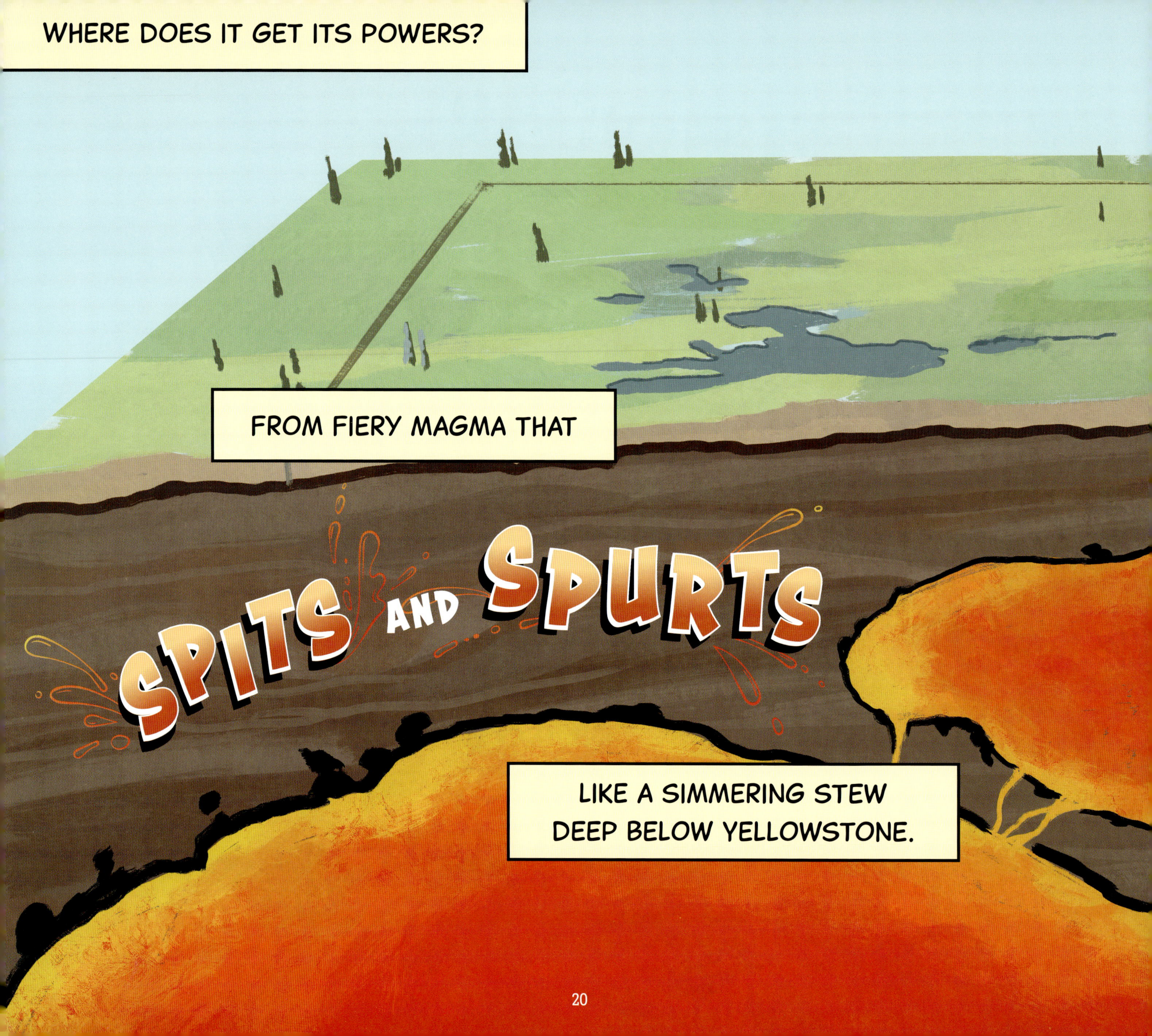

WHERE DOES IT GET ITS POWERS?

FROM FIERY MAGMA THAT

SPITS AND SPURTS

LIKE A SIMMERING STEW DEEP BELOW YELLOWSTONE.

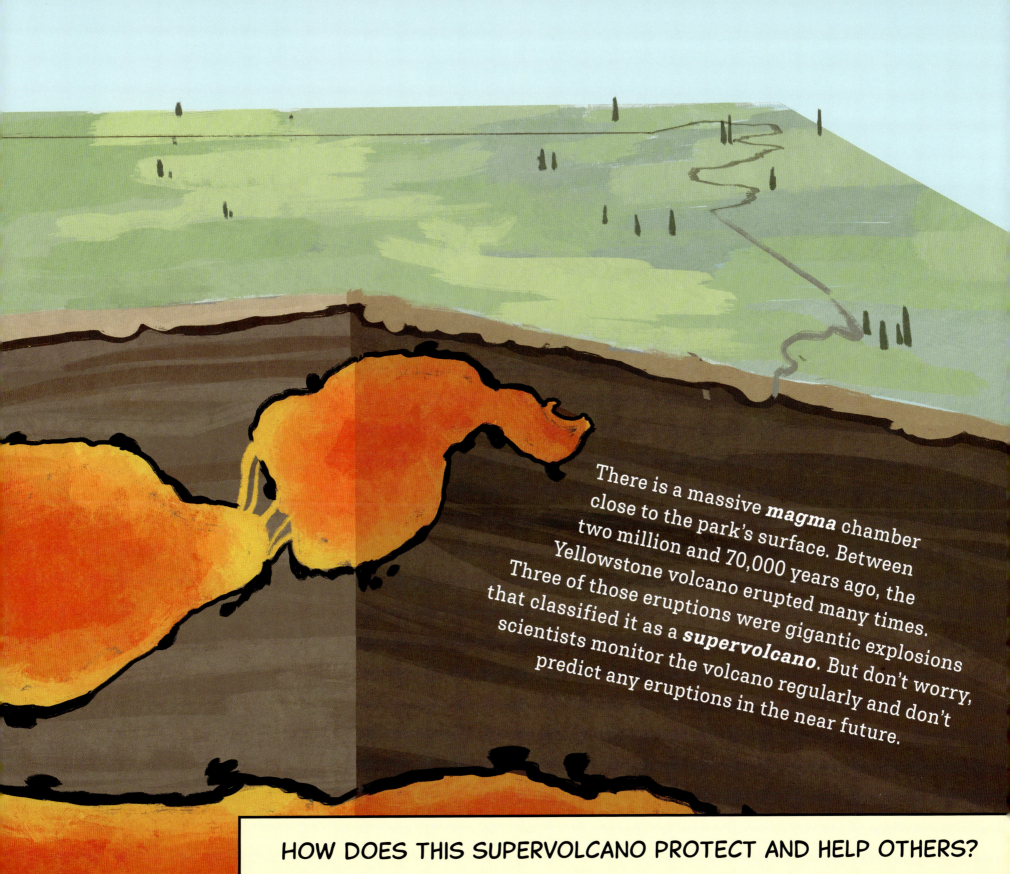

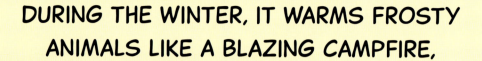

DURING THE WINTER, IT WARMS FROSTY ANIMALS LIKE A BLAZING CAMPFIRE,

Bison in search of a grassy meal can plow snow using their heads. As more snow falls, it becomes harder to clear the massive piles. The chilled bison then join deer and elk near the hydrothermal features to stay toasty warm.

MUNCH!

FEEDS HUNGRY GRAZERS BY UNCOVERING GRASS HIDDEN BENEATH THE SNOW,

Unique to Yellowstone, plants like Ross' bentgrass and Yellowstone sand verbena thrive in the tropical habitat created by the supervolcano. Attracted to the hot, thin soil surrounding Yellowstone's lakes and thermal features, they grow sturdy and strong.

AND MOISTENS AND HEATS PLANTS LIKE A NATURAL GREENHOUSE.

AND THE ENGINEER OF A FISHING HOLE FOR BIRDS TO PLUNGE INTO FOR FOOD.

PLUNK!

Yellowstone is known for long winters with frosty temperatures and deep snow. Fortunately, the supervolcano keeps sections of the park's lakes and rivers from freezing, providing a year-round eatery for trumpeter swans, eagles, and other hungry birds.

IT COOKS A FEAST FOR GRIZZLIES IN SPRING,

Not all animals survive the harsh winter. When spring arrives, hungry black bears and grizzlies emerge from *hibernation* and make their way to the thermal areas to enjoy a tasty barbeque.

YUM!

Tiny organisms called **thermophiles** thrive in the extreme heat of Yellowstone's hot springs. They are so small, you need a microscope to see them. Several types and colors of thermophiles live in different water temperatures. The different types pool together in rings, forming a vibrant rainbow of color.

The History of Yellowstone

Sitting atop the largest volcanic system in North America is a natural treasure—Yellowstone National Park.

Approximately two million years ago, the **hot spot** volcano we now call the Yellowstone Supervolcano blew its top. It exploded again about 1.3 million years ago, and a third time about 631,000 years ago.

Most volcanoes erupt out of cone-shaped mountains, but not the Yellowstone Supervolcano. Each time it erupted, it collapsed in on itself, creating a large volcanic crater called a **caldera**.

The Yellowstone Caldera is 1,500 square miles (3,880 square kilometers). It is mostly in Wyoming, but it also spans across parts of Montana and Idaho. While the Yellowstone Supervolcano is currently **dormant**, or sleeping, the magma chamber below remains restless.

Today, there are two areas called **resurgent domes** being pushed up by the moving magma underneath. This moving magma and the chamber's continuous heat is the power behind the splendor of Yellowstone.

For at least 11,000 years before it became a national park, **indigenous** tribes such as the Blackfeet, Crow, Nez Perce, Bannock, and Shoshone fished, hunted, and gathered plants on the land we now call Yellowstone.

They also mined obsidian rock, a volcanic glass formed when lava quickly cools. The indigenous peoples used it to make tools, arrowheads, and sharp blades for spears and knives.

Indigenous peoples are also credited with naming the area in the early 1800s after the yellow sandstone found along the banks of the Yellowstone River.

In 1871, a team of explorers and scientists traveled to Yellowstone to document its wonders through journals, artwork, and photographs. After their expedition, they convinced Congress to protect Yellowstone's marvels, making it America's first national park. The following year, President Ulysses S. Grant signed the Yellowstone National Park Protection Act declaring the park "For the Benefit and Enjoyment of the People."

A National Treasure

The landscape over the volcano consists of valleys, canyons, lakes, rivers, thermal areas, mountains, and forests.

Because of its fertile volcanic ash soil, 80% of Yellowstone is lush forest. Most of the trees are winter-hardy pines, but there are a few deciduous, or leafy, trees such as the quaking aspen.

Yellowstone is also blanketed with vibrant wildflowers—paintbrush, bluebells, shooting stars, yellow monkeyflower, and fireweed create a feast for the senses. Picking these wildflowers is against park rules, since many birds and animals dine on their seeds and berries for nourishment.

Nestled in Yellowstone's diverse habitat is an array of wildlife. Birds such as bald eagles, osprey, Canadian geese, mallard ducks, sandhill cranes, and mountain chickadees can be seen throughout the park. Its vast wilderness is also home to large mammals such as grey wolves, bighorn sheep, pronghorns, grizzly bears, bison, elk, and moose.

Additionally, Yellowstone shelters smaller mammals such as badgers, voles, red squirrels, rabbits, and yellow-bellied marmots. In its lakes and rivers, visitors can see beavers, river otters, cutthroat trout, American white pelicans, and trumpeter swans. Keep in mind while exploring the outdoors, including national parks, that **ecosystems** thrive on their own, and feeding the animals does more harm than good.

Yellowstone National Park is open year-round, and each season brings unique **flora** and **fauna**. People from all over the world flock to visit and enjoy this natural wonder. To preserve Yellowstone for future generations, remember to take only pictures, leave only footprints.

The Yellowstone League Of Superheroes

When Yellowstone was established as America's first national park, it was dedicated "for the benefit and enjoyment of the people." This remains true, but for this to continue, we, "the people," must take care of it.

With four distinct seasons of equal length, Yellowstone is one of the largest nearly undamaged **temperate ecosystems** on our planet. To protect it, we need a league of superheroes.

Leading this charge are the U.S. park rangers. Their main job is to protect and preserve the land and living creatures that make up Yellowstone. To ensure visitor safety, park rangers are in charge of medical response, search and rescue, law enforcement, and making sure visitors follow park rules. They also enjoy the responsibility of educating guests about Yellowstone's past, present, and future.

Another member of the league of superheroes is the National Park Service (NPS). As an agency of the federal government, the NPS has the difficult job of making the park accessible to visitors while protecting the fragile ecosystem. The NPS has placed boardwalks around the hydrothermal features to help guests safely enjoy the views without damaging these areas. They have designed programs to help protect wildlife such as grizzly bears, bison, trout, and trumpeter swans, which are being affected by **climate change**.

Scientists are also some of Yellowstone's superheroes. They study the supervolcano, thermal features, weather, flora, and fauna to help us better understand the park's ecosystem and preserve its natural resources. Geologists constantly monitor the volcano for signs of activity. If they ever have concerns about a possible eruption, the park will be closed immediately.

The League of Superheroes is recruiting you!

To preserve Yellowstone, we all must become stewards and protectors of the park. You can start by taking the Yellowstone Pledge:

"I pledge to protect Yellowstone National Park. I will act responsibly and safely, set a good example for others, and share my love of the park and all the things that make it special."

Caldera – a large crater formed when a volcano erupts and collapses in on itself.

Climate – the general weather conditions of a specific area over a period of time.

Climate change – changes in the general weather conditions of a geographic area over a period of time.

Dormant – not active now, but could become active later on.

Ecosystem – a geographic area made up of living things interacting with each other and their environment.

Eruption – the event of a volcano suddenly blasting or pouring out melted rock, hot gas, and ash.

Fauna – the animal wildlife of a geographic area.

Flora – the plants, trees, fungi, and bacteria of a geographic area.

Fumarole – an opening on the surface of a volcano where hot vapors and gases escape.

Geologist – a scientist who studies the Earth and what it is made of.

Geyser – an opening in the ground that shoots out hot water and steam.

Greenhouse – a building made of glass or plastic that traps the heat of the sun, creating an environment that is good for growing plants.

Hibernation – an inactive state animals go into during winter to survive cold temperatures and a lack of food.

Hot spot – an area under Earth's outer layer where magma that is hotter than the surrounding magma rises toward the Earth's surface, resulting in volcanic activity.

Hot spring – a natural pool of very hot water.

Hydrothermal – relating to hot water in the Earth's crust.

Indigenous – the earliest known peoples living in a particular region.

Magma – melted rock beneath the Earth's surface; when magma flows out from the Earth's surface it is called lava.

Mud pot – a hot spring filled with mud.

Resurgent dome – a bulge formed when the ground is lifted up by magma increasing beneath it.

Sulfuric acid – a dangerous chemical that can break down hard substances such as metal and rock; it is found in Yellowstone's hot springs, mud pots, and fumaroles and smells like rotten eggs.

Supervolcano – a volcano that has had an extremely large and explosive eruption. Other supervolcanoes include Lake Toba in Indonesia, Tamu Massif in Japan, and the Taupō Volcano in New Zealand.

Temperate ecosystem – an ecosystem with four seasons, cooler winters, and warmer summers.

Thermal – related to or caused by heat.

Thermophile – any organism that thrives in a very hot environment.

About the Author and Illustrator

SUZANNE JACOBS LIPSHAW is a children's book author and former elementary special education teacher passionate about growing young minds, engaging readers, and empowering student leaders. The proud momma of two grown boys, Suzanne lives in Waterford, Michigan with her husband and furry writing companion, Ziggy. When she's not dreaming up new writing projects, you can find her reading, kayaking, hiking, or practicing yoga. Contact her at Suzanne.Jacobs.Lipshaw@ScienceNaturally.com.

BRIE SCHMIDA is a children's illustrator and visual development artist based in California. As a farm girl turned artist, she has always been enchanted with nature in all its forms. When she isn't drawing, you may find her milking a goat, reading historical dramas, or tromping over hill and dale with her indefatigable dog, Olive.

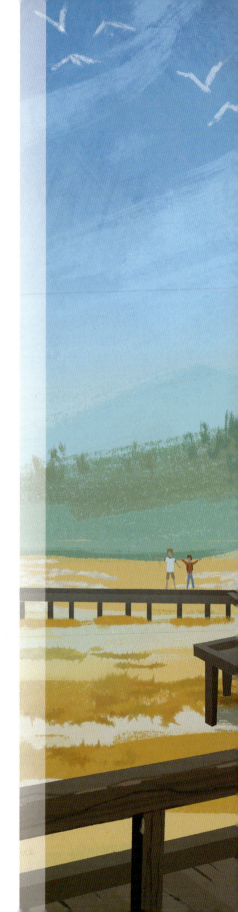